Celebrity Biographies

Rihanna
MUSIC MEGASTAR

BY MICHAEL A. SCHUMAN

Enslow Publishers, Inc.
40 Industrial Road
Box 398
Berkeley Heights, NJ 07922
USA
http://www.enslow.com

Library of Congress Cataloging-in-Publication Data

Schuman, Michael.
  Rihanna : music megastar / Michael A. Schuman.
       p. cm. — (Hot celebrity biographies)
  Includes index.
  Summary: "Read about Rihanna's life on Barbados, how she got her recording contract, and her life and charity work"—
    Provided by publisher.
  ISBN 978-0-7660-3871-4
  1. Rihanna, 1988—Juvenile literature. 2. Singers—Biography—Juvenile literature. I. Title.
  ML3930.R44S34 2011
  782.42164092—dc22
  [B]
            2010048145

Paperback ISBN: 978-1-59845-285-3

Printed in the United States of America

052011 Lake Book Manufacturing, Inc., Melrose Park, IL

10 9 8 7 6 5 4 3 2 1

To Our Readers: We have done our best to make sure all Internet Addresses in this book were active and appropriate when we went to press. However, the author and publisher have no control over and assume no liability for the material available on those Internet sites or on other Web sites they may link to. Any comments or suggestions can be sent by e-mail to comments@enslow.com or to the address on the back cover.

 Enslow Publishers, Inc., is committed to printing our books on recycled paper. The paper in every book contains 10% to 30% post-consumer waste (PCW). The cover board on the outside of each book contains 100% PCW. Our goal is to do our part to help young people and—the environment—too!

Cover Illustration: AP Images/Chris Pizzello.

Photos and Illustrations: AP Images/Chris Pizzello, p. 1; AP Images/Eric Jamison, p. 6; AP Images/Evan Agostini, pp. 14, 30; AP Images/Jason DeCrow, p. 25; AP Images/Jennifer Graylock, pp. 32, 34, 42; AP Images/Kathy Willens, p. 8; AP Images/Kevork Djansczian, pp. 17, 19, 28, 36 (right); AP Images/Lisa Rose, p. 26; AP Images/Lori Shepler, p. 36 (left); AP Images/Matt Sayles, pp 4, 40; AP Images/Roberto Pfeil, p. 18; AP Images/Sergio Dionisio, p. 12; AP Images/Tammie Arroyo, p. 10 (Rihanna photo); AP Images/Women's Wear Daily, p. 24; Artville, p. 10 (map).

Contents

Rihanna Arrives!

Rihanna sat in the audience in a floor-length pink gown. The date was September 9, 2007. She was surrounded by the best people in rock and pop music. The setting was the annual Video Music Awards (VMAs). She waited anxiously to hear who would win the award for Video of the Year.

Rihanna had already won a VMA award that night. It was for Monster Single of the Year for her song "Umbrella." But Video of the Year was the evening's biggest prize. Artists up for the honor included superstars Beyoncé, Justin Timberlake, Kanye West, and Amy Winehouse. The list also included Rihanna, who just two years earlier was a shy teenager from the Caribbean island of Barbados.

Finally, the time came to announce the big winner. Both live and television audiences were waiting. Then the name was announced: Rihanna for "Umbrella."

Rihanna beamed as she walked to the stage and accepted the award. Hip-hop legend Dr. Dre handed it to her.

◀ At awards shows like the 2007 Video Music Awards, celebrities like Rihanna walk the red carpet and pose for photos.

▲ Rihanna holds her award for Monster Single of the Year for her song "Umbrella" at the Video Music Awards on September 9, 2007.

Rihanna later said to *Entertainment Weekly*, "I was so honored. I could not believe that I won one of the biggest awards of the night, video of the year. Monster single of the year—I thought I had a chance. But video of the year was definitely the one I was like, there's no way. There are too many good videos and big artists in this category."

But just who was this award-winning nineteen-year-old? She has an exciting story to tell.

Island Girl

Robyn Rihanna Fenty was born in Saint Michael in Barbados on February 20, 1988. It is the largest parish, or region, of the country. (Instead of states, Barbados is made up of eleven parishes.) Her father, Ronald, worked in a clothing factory. Her mother, Monica, was an accountant. Monica later quit her job to open a clothing store. Monica is from Guyana, a nation in northern South America. Ronald is part Barbadian and part Irish.

Rihanna was neither rich nor poor. The Fenty family did not have a lot of money. But a lack of it was never a major problem.

That does not mean life was easy for Rihanna as a child. She was teased in school because of her light brown skin. She told *Entertainment Weekly*, "People hated me because I'm fair in complexion. I had to develop a thick skin because they would call me white."

Her troubles did not end when the school day was over. Her father had severe drug addictions. According to

▲ Rihanna sings the "Star-Spangled Banner" to kick off a Yankees-Mets baseball game on May 21, 2006.

Entertainment Weekly, Ronald was addicted to crack cocaine, marijuana, and alcohol.

This hurt his marriage. The couple constantly argued, which really stressed out Rihanna. Because of these problems, Rihanna was shy and liked being alone. She said, "I wouldn't cry. I wouldn't get upset." She continued, "It was just all in here," as she pointed to her head.

Rihanna detailed the trouble of living with her father to the *London Guardian*. She recalled:

> I didn't know what it was I was so scared of at first. I was very ignorant. I just saw what was going on. Heard the arguments. Then I was angry. I was: "Why are you doing this. This is not cool." I was, "Are you stupid? You know it's wrong, you see the effect it has on us." I could never understand why he wanted to continue.

As a result of the stress, Rihanna suffered painful headaches. Her mother thought she might have a brain tumor. A tumor is a swollen growth of tissue in the body. Such tumors often lead to cancer. Rihanna visited doctors many times. They gave her several CAT scans of the brain. CAT scans are similar to X-rays. Yet no doctor could find anything physically wrong with her.

MUSIC AND JOY

Music brought the young girl the most joy. She started singing to herself around age seven. She said to the *Honolulu Advertiser*, "Growing up, I always sang. But no one was ever really pushing me to do it. It was something that I wanted to do. So I developed a personal passion for it, fell in love with music and developed my own taste and style."

Not a lot of rock music is played in Barbados. Rihanna grew up listening to the reggae music native to the Caribbean. She also heard a lot of soca music.

BARBADOS

Most people in North America know of Barbados only as a warm-weather vacation destination. Barbados was a British colony for over three hundred years. It became an independent nation in 1966. Barbados maintains a strong connection to its British heritage. Residents speak English. Commuters ride in double-decker buses. The British game of cricket is the national sport.

▲ Rihanna at the World Music Awards in 2005.

Soca is not heard often in the United States. It is a combination of two musical styles. One is soul (the "so" in soca), or American soul music. The other is calypso (the "ca" in soca), a traditional Caribbean music. Calypso features a lot of steel drums, horns, and bass.

Rihanna was also able to listen to two types of music made popular by the African-American community. One was hip-hop. The other was light rhythm and blues. It is sung by artists such as Whitney Houston, Mariah Carey, and Destiny's Child.

When not singing, Rihanna played with her male relatives. Rihanna told the *Honolulu Advertiser* that with two brothers and thirteen male cousins she did not have much of a choice. "Me and [a] cousin were the only two girls, and we had to fight to defend ourselves because [the boys] didn't want us around. We wanted to do what they did. We wanted to climb trees. We wanted to fight. We wanted to catch animals."

CHANGES AT HOME
When Rihanna was about twelve, her parents split up for a short time. Soon afterwards, they moved back in together. They wanted to give their marriage another chance. They split and moved in together a few more times. Then they decided enough was enough. When Rihanna was fourteen, her parents divorced.

The divorce of one's parents can be difficult for teenagers to deal with. But things actually got better for Rihanna. Without the stress of seeing her parents constantly fight, Rihanna no longer had headaches. She stayed in touch with both parents. She did not blame her father's addictions for her parents' divorce. And through hard work, Ronald conquered his addictions. Rihanna said, "He got through it really well, actually." Today she and her father are close.

With things calming down at home after her parents' divorce, Rihanna could finally focus on herself.

▲ *Soca music is related to calypso music. Above, a boy performs in a calypso celebration in Great Britain.*

"Like a Star" at Fifteen

When she was fifteen, Rihanna did something unusual for a shy person. She formed a singing trio with two classmates. Singing in private was one thing. But performing for an audience meant people would judge her.

Rihanna was climbing out of her shell. She put her tomboy days behind her. She entered a school beauty pageant—and won! Rihanna admitted to the *London Guardian*, "It was very new and weird to me. I only started wearing make-up after I won [the] beauty pageant."

A GREAT BREAK

Many musical artists try for years to get discovered. They will make a demo, or demonstration recording, of their best performances. They will then send the demo to music producers, agents, and record labels. They hope to get discovered and hit the big time. However, most settle for playing local clubs and parties.

Then there are people like Rihanna, who get lucky. A songwriter and music producer named Evan Rogers and

RIHANNA IN ARMY FATIGUES

Rihanna once became a cadet in a program connected to the Barbados army. Her drill sergeant, Shontelle Layne, was three years older than her. By coincidence, Shontelle also became a professional singer. What were the chances that one future pop singer would command another one in an army program?

Shontelle told the British Broadcasting Company of London, "We were both in the cadets together—it wasn't compulsory or anything. But picture me and Rihanna in combat boots and fatigues crawling through mud and things like that."

Shontelle adds on her Web site that Rihanna was "a good cadet, though there was one occasion when I had to make her drop and give me ten push-ups. We laugh about it now. I think she's forgiven me."

▲ *Before she became a singer, Shontelle (above) gave Rihanna orders in a youth military program.*

his wife took a vacation to Barbados in 2003. Rogers had worked with another songwriter and producer named Carl Sturken. Together, they produced hits for Christina Aguilera and American Idol winners Ruben Studdard and Kelly Clarkson.

The mother of one of Rihanna's friends knew Rogers. Rihanna's friend's mother told Rogers about a talented trio in Barbados. As a favor, Rogers said he would let them audition. Rihanna knew it was a chance few are given. She told writer Sylvia Patterson that she was "so nervous, this was my connection to the big world that was so unreachable."

She entered Rogers's suite wearing pink Capris and a pink shirt. It turned out she had nothing to worry about. Rogers was wowed by her poise and talent. He remembered, "The minute Rihanna walked into the room, it was like the other two girls didn't exist."

SINGING FOR ROGERS

Rihanna sang two numbers. One was Mariah Carey's "Hero." The other was Destiny's Child's "Emotion." Rogers said, "She carried herself like a star even when she was 15. But the killer was when she opened her mouth to sing ['Emotion']. She was a little rough around the edges, but she had this edge to her voice."

Rogers called Rihanna back for a second audition. He was so impressed that he invited her to his home in Stamford, Connecticut. There they would record a demo. Rihanna was only fifteen and still in high school. The demo would take a long time to record. Rihanna's mother said that was okay with her—as long as her daughter worked on the demo between school sessions.

Soon, Rihanna and her mother packed their bags and traveled to the United States.

4 "I Signed Her in One Day"

For the next year Rihanna and her mother were the airlines' best friends. They made many trips from Barbados to Connecticut. Rogers and Rihanna worked for months to make a top quality demo.

Rihanna's mother recognized how hard Rihanna and Rogers were working. When Rihanna turned sixteen, her mother allowed her to move in with Rogers and his wife. Tutors came to the Rogers's home to help Rihanna finish her high school work.

Moving to another country was a brave move. But Rihanna was determined to follow her dream. She recalled, "When I left Barbados, I didn't look back. I wanted to do what I had to do, even if it meant moving to America."

THE DEMO IS COMPLETE

After about a year, Rihanna's demo was finished. It contained four songs. One was a hip-hop and reggae-style dance number titled "Pon de Replay." It's about a girl who likes to dance to her favorite song. The title might sound like gibberish but it makes perfect sense to a girl from Barbados.

Rihanna told kidzworld.com, "It's just language that we speak in Barbados. It's broken English. Pon is 'on.' De means 'the,' so it's just basically telling the DJ to put my song on the replay."

▲ *Rihanna (right) always loved Beyoncé's music. Later, when Rihanna got famous, she was able to meet Beyoncé.*

In January 2005, Rogers and Sturken sent the demo to several people in the music industry. They did not have to wait long for a reply. Within weeks, they heard from Def Jam Recordings. Def Jam's president, hip-hop star Jay-Z, wanted Rihanna to audition. So she traveled to Jay-Z's office.

▲ As "Pon de Replay" became a hit, Rihanna toured the world performing songs from her first album, Music of the Sun.

Rihanna later recalled, "And that's when I really got nervous. I was like: 'Oh God, he's right there. I can't look. I can't look. I can't look.'"

But she did look. And she did sing. Rihanna belted out the Whitney Houston version of the Isley Brothers' song "For the Love of You." She then sang "Pon de Replay" and another song written by Rogers and Sturken, "The Last Time."

IMPRESSING JAY-Z

Jay-Z was amazed. He said, "I signed her in one day. It took me two minutes to see she was a star."

Rihanna and Jay-Z did not waste time. They got busy recording Rihanna's first album. It was released just half a year later, in August 2005. Its title is *Music of the Sun*.

Its first single was "Pon de Replay." The single reached number two on the Hot 100 songs chart published by *Billboard* magazine. *Billboard* is well respected in the music industry. The album *Music of the Sun* reached number ten on *Billboard*'s top albums chart.

▲ *At the beginning of 2005, Jay-Z agreed to put out Rihanna's albums. Three years later, he was onstage with her when she accepted a Grammy award for her song "Umbrella."*

Not all music critics liked Rihanna or the song. Some said she was a Beyoncé wanna-be. Others said she would never have another hit. Rihanna remembered, "A lot of people said I was going to be a one-hit wonder. But I worked my hardest to prove them wrong."

A SMASH HIT

Rihanna's next album, *A Girl Like Me*, came out in April 2006. The songs on the album were mainly about things teenage girls go through, such as crushes, falling in love, and dealing with cheating boyfriends.

The album's first single, "SOS," is about a girl who is deeply in love with a boy. She is so in love with him that she feels out of control.

"SOS" samples a techno-pop hit record titled "Tainted Love." "Tainted Love" was released in 1981 by the British duo Soft Cell. Rihanna admitted, "I didn't know

TOURING WITH GWEN

In 2006, Rihanna toured with superstar Gwen Stefani. Rihanna was the opening act and Stefani was the headliner.

One reason for the tour was to make people aware of *Music of the Sun*. But there was another purpose. It helped Rihanna become familiar with rock music.

She posted on her Web site, "Coming from Barbados, I hadn't heard that much rock music. Touring with Gwen changed my perspective. So, when I was discussing this project with L.A. Reid, chairman of Island Def Jam Records, I made sure to say I want to experiment with some rock."

about Soft Cell or any of those older artists, until I moved to America, y'know, and I put that in my music. I fused that with pop and R&B and made a new song."

"SOS" was a smash. It was Rihanna's first song to reach number one on the *Billboard* Hot 100 chart. Her second single from *A Girl Like Me* was titled "Unfaithful."

Unlike the up-tempo "SOS," "Unfaithful" is a ballad. Rihanna sings about the feelings of a girl who has a boyfriend. Yet she is falling in love with someone new. She feels horrible for what her new feelings must be doing to her boyfriend. Like "SOS," "Unfaithful" was a hit. It reached number six on the Billboard Hot 100 chart.

Meanwhile, *A Girl Like Me* peaked at number five on the *Billboard* albums chart. As for the people who said she would never have a hit after "Pon de Replay," Rihanna had proven them wrong.

"Umbrella" Conquers the World

Still a teenager, Rihanna was making an adjustment that gives even many adults trouble. She was becoming famous.

She learned who her real friends are. She said, "When I signed my recording deal, a few fake friends and I parted ways." She added, "I gained some [friends] who wanted to get close to me because of the deal, so they had to go as well."

Rihanna credits her mother with keeping her grounded. She told writer Amina Taylor:

> My mom raised me to be a child and know my place, but also to think like a woman. She never held back from me in terms of being too young to know certain things, so fortunately I am very mature for my age. In this business you have to work with the things that get thrown your way, the good, the bad, and the ugly.

RUMORS

It did not take long for an "ugly" thing to raise its head. Rihanna had become a star very quickly. Because of that,

BELIEVE FOUNDATION

Rihanna's fame also allowed her to do good things. She explained, "When I was young and I would watch television and I would see all the children suffering. I always said, `When I grow up, I want to help.'"

So in 2006 she started a group called Believe Foundation. Its purpose is to help children with life-threatening diseases, especially leukemia. Leukemia is cancer of the bone marrow. Bone marrow is a tissue found in bone cavities. It is responsible for making red and white blood cells. For some leukemia victims, a bone marrow transplant is truly the difference between life and death.

The Believe Foundation Web site says, "Believe gives children a chance to not only survive, but thrive in a world where many will never receive the medical attention, school supplies, toys and clothes that they deserve."

To help raise money for the Believe Foundation, Rihanna has given benefit concerts and donated items for celebrity auctions. She even helped find a blood marrow donor for a mother stricken with leukemia.

some bloggers spread rumors that she was dating Jay-Z. They wrote that that was the reason for her success. At the time, Jay-Z was dating his future wife, Beyoncé. Some said there was a feud between Rihanna and Beyoncé.

None of that was true. Rihanna told writer Monica Corcoran, "I felt self-conscious around him until he [Jay-Z] took me aside and said that I just had to ignore it."

Early in 2006 Rihanna moved out of Rogers's home and rented an apartment in Los Angeles. She was still a teenager. Rogers and Jay-Z were concerned how she would get by on her own.

▲ Rihanna helped promote J.C. Penney products. She also attended a J.C. Penney fundraiser in New York City on March 2, 2006, which benefited the group Broadway Cares.

Jay-Z told writer Margeaux Watson, "The biggest advice I can give her is to keep her circle tight, because she can't control anything else outside of that. She can't control people's opinions of her records or what's being said on the blogs . . . But if she has the proper friends, she won't get caught up in the wild-child lifestyle."

HELPING SELL PRODUCTS

Celebrities often endorse, or advertise, products or services. Companies pay the celebrities for appearing in their ads.

Rihanna's first endorsement was for Secret Body Spray. The company believed teenage girls would buy their body spray if Rihanna represented it. Secret Body Spray also sponsored, or helped pay the expenses for, the first national concert tour that was headlined by Rihanna.

Soon, other companies wanted Rihanna to promote their products. She made endorsement deals with Nike sportswear, the department store J.C. Penney, Clinique cosmetics, and Gucci handbags. Furthermore, Rihanna drummed up publicity for her native country. She appeared in ads for the Barbados Tourism Board.

When not working for her favorite charity or a sponsor, Rihanna spent much of 2006 headlining the Rock the Block tour. She was also in the recording studio making her third album. In addition, Rihanna found time to appear in a movie. It is a high school cheerleading comedy titled *Bring It On: All or Nothing*. Rihanna has a brief appearance playing herself.

Then in November 2006 she embarked on another tour. This one took place in the United Kingdom, where she shared the stage with the Pussycat Dolls. It ended in February 2007. Shortly afterward, her third album was released.

▶ *On April 25, 2006, the day before her album* A Girl Like Me *went on sale, Rihanna performed on MTV's Total Request Live.*

A NEW LOOK

With the release of her third album, Rihanna changed her appearance. Anyone expecting to see the perky, long-haired Rihanna was shocked. She cut her long brown locks and dyed her new short hairstyle black. She wore less conservative clothes. That gave her a rebellious image. Now that she was nineteen, Rihanna wanted to be seen as a young adult. The title of her third album summed up her changes. It was called *Good Girl Gone Bad*.

▲ *By the time of the Nickelodeon Kids' Choice Awards on March 31, 2007, Rihanna had a short hairstyle to show off.*

However, the first single of her third album was not about rebellion. It is a song about friendship titled "Umbrella." It also featured a rap by Jay-Z. In the song, Rihanna tells a friend she will always share her umbrella with her when it's raining. She means that no matter what, she will always stand by her friend.

In 2007, "Umbrella" became a huge summer hit. It was number one for seven weeks on *Billboard*'s Hot 100 chart. The Web site allmusic.com said "Umbrella" was "her best [song] to date." In fact, the entire album received good reviews. Music critic Neil Drumming wrote, "*Good Girl Gone Bad* is a thrilling throwback to more than a decade ago." The album reached number two on *Billboard*'s weekly list of top 200 albums.

After "Umbrella," seven more cuts from *Good Girl Gone Bad* were released as singles. One, "Don't Stop the Music," reached number three on the *Billboard* chart. It is a lively number about having fun on the dance floor. A year after the album came out, it was released again as *Good Girl Gone Bad: Reloaded* and included three more songs. One of them was "Disturbia." It is about the anxious feelings people sometimes get. "Disturbia" reached number one.

OFF TO TOKYO

Rihanna was hardly done with charity work. In July 2007, she flew to Tokyo. There she sang in the Live Earth concert. It was one of a series of concerts that took place across the world. Its purpose was to make people familiar with the problem of climate change.

After the success of *Good Girl Gone Bad*, Rihanna had reached the status of superstar. In September 2007 she headlined the *Good Girl Gone Bad* tour. It lasted over a year off and on and included concerts around the world.

Diva!

The year 2007 ended with exciting news for Rihanna. Her song "Umbrella" was nominated for a 2008 Grammy, a top music award. It was up for record of the year.

Rihanna performed two songs on the televised Grammys: "Umbrella" and "Don't Stop the Music." While she did not win Record of the Year, she did receive a Grammy in a different category: Best Rap/Sung Collaboration, for her work with Jay-Z on "Umbrella." During her acceptance speech, Rihanna shared her excitement with her father. She said, "Dad, I know I promised you I'd give you my first Grammy, but we're going to have to fight for this one!"

The Grammy was not a win for Rihanna alone. The entire nation of Barbados celebrated with her. Barbados's Prime Minister David Thompson sent a video message congratulating her. Thompson said to the media, "Words cannot express the excitement and pride felt by Barbadians around the world when our superstar Rihanna won her first Grammy Award after being discovered merely two years ago."

◀ *Rihanna dances during her high-energy performance at the 2008 Grammy Awards.*

HER FRIENDS AND BOYFRIENDS

With her talent, looks, and poise, Rihanna was now one of the most popular women in show business. But what kind of men did she like to date? She told Monica Corcoran she likes men with humility. She said, "If a guy is hot and he knows—forget it. I hate arrogance." She added, "I like facial hair and a guy who dresses rugged."

She went on to tell Corcoran, "I have three girlfriends and about 20 guy friends. I love listening to guy talk because I

▼ *Rihanna and Taylor Swift (right) appear on MTV's* Total Request Live *in June 2008.*

learn a lot. Here's the key: You can't lower your standards for a guy because he won't respect you and he'll tell his friends. You always have to stick up for yourself and speak your mind."

Naturally, rumors about Rihanna's social life spread in gossip publications and on Web sites. By the spring of 2008 there were reports that she was dating a lot of actors. The list included Shia LaBeouf and Josh Hartnett. Rihanna said those reports were not true. But before long it was clear she had a steady boyfriend: hip-hop artist Chris Brown.

RIHANNA DAY

With her Grammy win fresh news, Rihanna was honored by her home country. The government of Barbados declared February 21, 2008—one day after her 20th birthday—"Rihanna Day." Thousands of people gathered in Independence Square in Bridgetown, the nation's capital. Many carried umbrellas in honor of her hit song. Rihanna was the center of attention as she stood next to Prime Minister Thompson.

The prime minister proudly said, ". . . the Government of Barbados designates Robyn Rihanna Fenty an honorary Youth and Cultural Ambassador of this country." The people screamed and cheered, and Rihanna returned the favor by giving a free concert.

CRITICS

Most people in Barbados and the rest of the world admired her. Her fans called her Ri-Ri as a fun nickname. But Rihanna did have critics. Some Barbadians felt she did not set a good example for young people.

◄Rihanna attended a party celebrating the beginning of Gucci's Tattoo Heart Collection.

One reason was because a photograph of Rihanna wearing a small swimsuit appeared in a Barbados newspaper. Rihanna explained to the BBC that the photo was taken at the beach. She said that such swimsuits are appropriate for the beach. She added that the photographer took her picture without her knowledge.

She said, "There were call-in (radio) programs about it. It was a big deal for, like, three weeks straight— talking about I'm not setting a good example."

Rihanna emphasized that the opposite was true. "I don't like to wear things too skimpy . . . That's what I admire so much about Alicia Keys. She became so successful off of just her music. She was really conservative about her style at first."

Rihanna took a break from her solo tour to join the *Glow in the Dark* tour. It starred Kanye West and other hip-hop performers such as Lupe Fiasco, N.E.R.D., and Nas.

"JUST STAND UP"

It is hard for Rihanna to say no to charities. In August she joined artists including Beyoncé, Mariah Carey, and Fergie to record a charity single titled, "Just Stand Up." It was to benefit a campaign called Stand Up to Cancer. Rihanna returned to the *Good Girl Gone Bad* tour in late October. However, she took time to be the spokesperson for Gucci's first United Nations Children's Fund.

Gucci is known for making fashions that only wealthy people can afford. Yet Gucci works with several charities. In December 2008, Rihanna appeared in advertisements for Gucci's Tattoo Heart campaign. Tattoo Heart helps bring relief to African children stricken with the AIDS/HIV virus.

With all Rihanna's hard work and success, it was little wonder that *Entertainment Weekly* writer Margeaux Watson called her "Diva of the Year" for 2008. Some take the term "diva" to mean a person who expects to always get what she wants. But Watson meant it as a compliment. She wrote, "Rihanna's newfound staying power is nothing short of remarkable."

With things going so well, who could have predicted that a dark and frightening incident was on the horizon?

The Dark Side and the Bright Side

As 2008 turned into 2009, everything seemed promising for Rihanna. She was nominated for two more Grammy awards. But shortly before the Grammys were to take place in February 2009, Rihanna canceled her appearance. Journalists wondered what was wrong. It was not like Rihanna to miss an important event.

There were rumors that she and her boyfriend Chris Brown had had a violent fight. Rihanna stayed out of the public spotlight for weeks. Then on March 5, everyone learned that the rumors were true. Brown was arrested for assaulting and threatening Rihanna.

To make matters worse, a gossip Web site got hold of a police department photo. The photo had been taken for evidence against Brown. It featured a close-up of Rihanna's face with scratches, swelling, and bruises. Rihanna did not make a public statement. But Brown said to the press, "Words cannot begin to express how sorry and saddened I am over what transpired."

◀ *At the end of 2009, a year in which she had to deal with Chris Brown's abuse, Rihanna was honored as a* Glamour *magazine* Woman of the Year.

BACK TO WORK

While Rihanna stayed out of the public eye, she did return to recording and video studios. She began recording a new album. She also appeared in Kanye West's music video for his song "Paranoid." Then she, West, and Jay-Z worked together on a hip-hop song titled "Run This Town." It is about power in the world of hip-hop music. "Run This Town" reached number two on the *Billboard* Hot 100 chart.

▼ *During the summer of 2009, Rihanna had to deal with the felony assault case against her ex-boyfriend Chris Brown. A felony is a very serious crime.*

On June 22, Chris Brown had his day in court. He pleaded guilty to felony assault. It means he caused bodily injury to a person. He did not have to go to jail as punishment.

But Brown was punished in other ways. He was put on five years' probation. That meant he would be free if he did not break any law for five years. If he did break a law while on probation, he could be sentenced to a stiff prison term.

In addition, Brown was forced to enroll in a counseling program. Its purpose was to help people guilty of domestic violence. He also had to perform 180 hours of community service as part of his sentence.

BACK IN THE PUBLIC EYE

On September 11, Rihanna performed at a charity concert organized by Jay-Z. The date was the eighth anniversary of the 2001 terrorist attacks on New York City and Washington, D.C. Jay-Z titled the concert "Answer the Call." Money raised at the event went to the New York Police and Fire Widows' and Children's Benefit Fund.

On September 14, Rihanna made her first public television appearance since she was beaten. The setting was *The Tonight Show with Jay Leno*. There she, Kanye West, and Jay-Z performed "Run This Town." Then on the November 2, 2009, airing of the television program *Good Morning America*, Rihanna broke her silence.

RIHANNA'S LAW

Even though Rihanna did not speak about the incident, others spoke for her. Many felt the beating was bad enough. But they thought releasing the photo was humiliating. Some formed a celebrity-rights advocacy group, called STOParazzi. The group nickname is a pun on paparazzi. "Paparazzi" is the informal name given to photographers who take candid pictures of celebrities. Some of them can be very embarrassing.

STOParazzi worked on making a law against releasing photos that take advantage of crime victims. They called it Rihanna's Law. However, it has not yet become a law. Its supporters are still working on making it official.

She was interviewed by the show's host, Diane Sawyer. Rihanna said that at first she was blinded by love—so much so that she went back to Brown soon after he had beaten her. She told Sawyer, "It's pretty natural for that to be the first reaction. The moment the physical wounds go away, you want the memories to go away."

Rihanna confessed that she made a mistake by getting back together with Brown. Rihanna said, "When I realized that my selfish decision for love could result in some young girl getting killed, I could not be easy with that." At that point, she had broken up with Brown for good.

Rihanna got busy promoting her fourth album, released in November. It was titled *Rated R*. It reached number four on the *Billboard* top albums chart in its first week out.

The songs showed a dark side of Rihanna. Many of the lyrics were angry and bitter. Some critics said the songs on the album were about her assault by Chris Brown. The reviews were mostly positive. Music critic Ed Potton called it "the best record she's made."

Five singles were released from the album. One, "Rude Boy," reached number one on *Billboard*'s Hot 100 chart. It was her sixth number one song in the United States.

Then Rihanna won her second and third Grammys at the 2010 awards. "Run This Town" won honors for both Best Rap Song and Best Rap/Sung Collaboration.

LAST GIRL ON EARTH

Rihanna was back. She embarked on her next tour on April 16. It was titled *Last Girl on Earth*. The tour took her to cities in Europe, Asia, and North America.

She told Kevin Frazier of *Entertainment Tonight* that she likes to think of herself as the last girl on Earth. That is so she can live life as she wants—not on how others think about her.

Now that the abusive relationship with Chris Brown was over, Rihanna was ready to move on. In the summer of 2010, she released another song that became a smash. It is a duet with rapper Eminem titled "Love The Way You Lie."

The song is about a man who acts violently against his girlfriend. Many were surprised that Rihanna took part in the song. After all, she had just gotten out of a violent relationship. Some critics answered that she wanted to make other women aware of abuse.

In September, her new single "Only Girl (In the World)" was released. It soon hit number one. Like "Don't Stop the Music," it is fast paced. Rihanna asks her boyfriend to make her feel like she's the only girl in the world. In the song's video, she sports yet

◄ Eminem sang with Rihanna on "Love the Way You Lie,"—a song of his about a physically abusive relationship.

another look. Rihanna had grown her hair long again, and dyed it a deep, dark red.

Then on November 12, her fifth studio album, *Loud*, was released. Unlike her previous two albums, *Loud* has a party feel. In an interview with Gil Kaufman of MTV, Rihanna tells her fans to "get LOUD everybody, get crazy, get excited, cuz I'm pumped. I'm just gonna be ME, cuz that's what u guys love the most, and that's what makes me feel best. Just being normal, normal for me is LOUD! Sassy, fun, flirty, energetic."

The reviews of *Loud* were mostly positive. Shortly afterward, the next single from *Loud* was released. It is titled "What's My Name?" It's a romantic number in which she sings about much how she loves her boyfriend. Rihanna shares vocals with Canadian rapper Drake. It soon became Rihanna's eighth number one song on the *Billboard* Hot 100 chart. A few weeks later, "Only Girl (In the World)" became her ninth number one song. That was unusual because it was released before "What's My Name?"

Rihanna has since shown that she can be creative outside music. She authored a photograph-filled book, published in the fall of 2010. Titled simply *Rihanna*, it tells the story of her first solo tour. Around the same time, she began filming the science fiction movie *Battleship*. She plays a naval officer who uses warships to fight invading aliens.

◀ *Rihanna signed copies of her book* Rihanna *at the 5th Avenue Barnes & Noble in New York City on October 27, 2010.*

Rihanna has also shown she has business sense. In November 2010, she started Rihanna Entertainment. With her own company, she can control how all her products are used. These include her music, movies, books, and even fashion and perfume. She told writer Jerry Shriver of *USA Today*, "Business is something I need to be a lot more serious about. I feel, like, really old doing it. It has made me grow up."

Rihanna has faced her share of ups and downs, including winning the Grammy for Best Dance Recording for "Only Girl (In the World)" in 2011. Now that she has branched out, the wisest question is not what will Rihanna sing next. It's, what will she do next?

Timeline

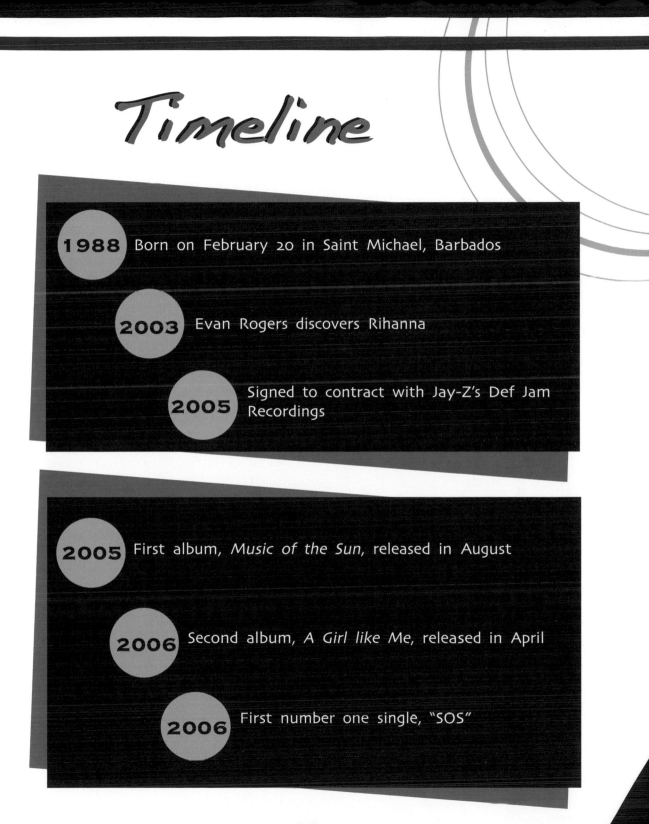

1988 Born on February 20 in Saint Michael, Barbados

2003 Evan Rogers discovers Rihanna

2005 Signed to contract with Jay-Z's Def Jam Recordings

2005 First album, *Music of the Sun*, released in August

2006 Second album, *A Girl like Me*, released in April

2006 First number one single, "SOS"

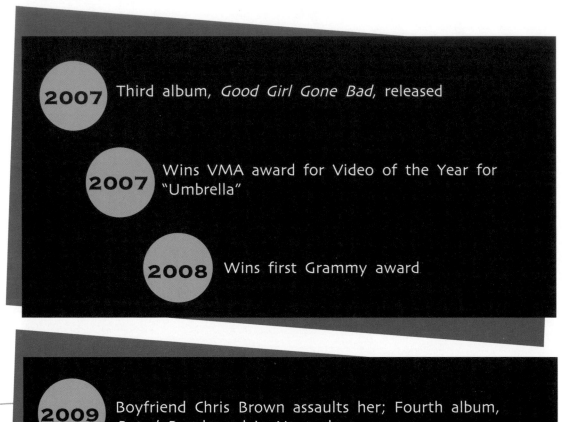

2007 Third album, *Good Girl Gone Bad*, released

2007 Wins VMA award for Video of the Year for "Umbrella"

2008 Wins first Grammy award

2009 Boyfriend Chris Brown assaults her; Fourth album, *Rated R*, released in November

2010 Fifth album, *Loud*, released in November; starts own business, Rihanna Entertainment; book, *Rihanna*, is released; ninth single hits number one

2011 Wins Grammy for Best Dance Recording for "Only Girl (In the World)"

Further Info

Books

Frank, Mary Kate. *Rihanna* (Today's Superstars). New York: Gareth Stevens Publishing, 2009.

Howse, Jennifer. *Rihanna* (Remarkable People). New York: Weigl Publishers, 2009.

Krumenauer, Heidi. *Rihanna* (Blue Banner Biographies). Hockessin, Del.: Mitchell Lane Publishers, 2008.

Internet Addresses

Rihanna's Allmusic.com Page
   http://allmusic.com/cg/amg.dll?p=amg&sql=11:3ifyxqesldae

Rihanna's Believe Foundation
   http://www.believerihanna.com/

Rihanna's Def Jam Recordings Site
   http://www.islanddefjam.com/artist/home.aspx?artistID=7366

Rihanna's Official Web site
   http://www.rihannanow.com/

Selected Discography

SINGLES RELEASED IN THE UNITED STATES

This list is of recordings by Rihanna alone or featuring her and other artists. Listed is the highest position each song reached on *Billboard* magazine's Hot 100 chart.

2005
"Pon de Replay" — #2
"If It's Lovin' that You Want" — #36

2006
"SOS" — #1 for three weeks
"Unfaithful" — #6
"Break It Off" with Sean Paul — #9

2007
"Umbrella" with Jay-Z — #1 for seven weeks
"Shut Up and Drive" —#15
"Hate That I Love You" featuring Ne-Yo — #7
"Don't Stop the Music" — #3

2008
"Take a Bow" — #1 for 1 week
"Disturbia" — #1 for 2 weeks
"Rehab" — #18
"Live Your Life" by T.I. featuring Rihanna — #1 for 6 weeks
"If I Never See Your Face Again" Maroon 5 with Rihanna — #51

2009
"Run This Town" Jay-Z featuring Rihanna and Kanye West — #2
"Hard" featuring Jeezy — #8

2010
"Rude Boy" — #1 for 5 weeks
"Love the Way You Lie" by Eminem with Rihanna — #1 for 7 weeks
"Rockstar 101" with Slash — #64
"Only Girl (In the World)" —#1 for 1 week
"What's My Name?" featuring Drake — #1 for 1 week

2011
"All of the Lights" by Kanye West with Rihanna — #31

STUDIO ALBUMS

Listed is the highest position each album reached on *Billboard*s Hot 100.

2005
Music of the Sun, #10

2006
A Girl Like Me, #5

2007
Good Girl Gone Bad, #2

2009
Rated R, #4

2010
Loud, #3

Glossary

audition—To try out for a part or contract in the performing arts, such as singing, dancing, or acting.

bloggers—Persons who publish Web logs, or "blogs," on the Internet.

CAT scan—A medical procedure that presents a picture of the inside of the body, similar to an X-ray.

collaboration—A project in which two or more people work together.

demo—A demonstration tape, or a recording of a musician's songs, made in hopes of getting a record contract.

endorsement—Promoting a product or service by giving it one's approval.

leukemia—Cancer of bone marrow.

music producer—A person who pays for and oversees the making of a record.

paparazzi—A general name given for people who make money taking candid pictures of celebrities.

parish—A region. In Barbados, any of 11 official regions similar to states in the United States.

Index